Henrietta
  What a [blessing you]
have been to me!
  Hope you will enjoy
my book.
  May God richly bless
you and all of yours!
  Best Wishes Both Now and
      For Always

    Wilma A. Hudgins
    Aydelott

I Saw My God Today While Walking The Path Of Life

Celebrated in free verse by

WILMA A. HUDGINS

> Please make the following corrections:
> P. 50 should read I Corinthians 12:5 (NIV)
> P. 57 should read (NCV) instead of (NIV)
> P. 99 Psalm 19:21 should read Proverbs 19:21

Bloomington, IN Milton Keynes, UK

AuthorHouse™
1663 Liberty Drive, Suite 200
Bloomington, IN 47403
www.authorhouse.com
Phone: 1-800-839-8640

AuthorHouse™ UK Ltd.
500 Avebury Boulevard
Central Milton Keynes, MK9 2BE
www.authorhouse.co.uk
Phone: 08001974150

©2007 Wilma A. Hudgins. All rights reserved.

No part of this book may be reproduced, stored in a retrieval system, or transmitted by any means without the written permission of the author.

First published by AuthorHouse 5/9/2007

ISBN: 978-1-4259-8001-6 (sc)

Library of Congress Control Number: 2006910756
Printed in the United States of America
Bloomington, Indiana

This book is printed on acid-free paper.

Scripture references designated NIV are taken from The Holy Bible, New International Version, 1973, 1978, 1984 International Bible Society. Used by permission of Zondervan Bible Publishers.

Scripture references designated NCV are quoted from The Holy Bible, New Century Version, copyright 2005 by Thomas Nelson, Inc. Used by permission of Zondervan Bible Publishers.

Scripture references designated KJV are quoted from The Holy Bible, King James Version

DEDICATED

To my children, James, Timothy, and Melanie, and to their respective families who constantly shower me with abundant love, encouragement, and support. They give me great joy, and teach me many lessons as I walk this path called life.

SPECIAL THANKS

A very sincere thanks goes to each and every one of my readers who has spoken to me in complimentary terms concerning my writing. Your words gave me special encouragement. Without them this book would never have been attempted!

A super thanks goes to my sister, Clara A. Shannon, who very willingly, patiently, and freely gave of her time and effort to proof read and critique my poems, through several months, as I was preparing them for publication.

Rachel Reed, an English major, at Lipscomb University, read part of my manuscript and used her expertise to update some of my outdated and pesky punctuation. Thanks again!

I remember, with pleasure, T. Romaine, an Instructor at the Renaissance Center, in Dickson, Tennessee, who first told me that my poetry was worthy of publication. Of course, that inspired me to continue writing.

As I grew up in the 1930's and 40's computers were nonexistent. My two daughters-in-law, Joyce Hudgins and Lesley Hudgins, are helping me to become somewhat computer literate, in order to expedite my written work. Joyce placed all my poems for this book on to a CD for me to send to the publisher. Thanks!!! Just one more way in which my daughters-in-law continue to endear themselves to me.

Much grateful appreciation goes to Bradley Martin, editor of the Hickman County Times, Centerville, Tennessee, for publishing my work in the Times. And what an honor to have him write the information for the back cover of my book.

Thanks, and thanks again for the kind words in the Foreword Section, written by Travis Irwin. What a great friend and treasured gospel minister he is to us who attend worship services where he preaches.

The AuthorHouse staff was exceptionally patient, professional, kind, and understanding as we worked together toward accomplishing the task of bringing this book to the point of publication. I now hold a new and somewhat enlightened respect for book publishers.

May God continue to pour out His blessings upon us all, is my fervent prayer!

FOREWORD

Poetry is usually about people, places or things. But I think poetry is more. Poetry is about its author. This poetry is no different.

The poetry contained herein is about nature, the spacious creation, God, family, morality, people, and other wonderful subjects, but it's really more about Wilma Hudgins. Wilma's life is worth a book itself. Her life is one of teaching, mothering and ladies' classes. And her poetry tells us about her. Her personality and her values are wonderfully depicted in her poetry. You will enjoy reading her poems and you will enjoy seeing into her heart at the same time. You will find that many of her values are also your values. You feel a commonality with her and a warm spot in your heart for her verse. May this collection be a launch pad to others.

TRAVIS IRWIN
Friend and Minister
9/24/06

PREFACE

A special thanks for purchasing my book. Most of these poems have been written and published in the Hickman County Times in 2005 and '06. However, a few of them were written in previous years or were recently written just for this book.

I have written in free verse – meaning I have not consistently depended on any rhyme patterns, line length or stanza shape to convey my intended thoughts to the reader.

I grew up in the 1930's and 40's. Therefore the convictions and viewpoints in my current writing does sometimes reflect that day and time instead of today's prevailing thought. In those cases I trust you will enjoy the nostalgic memories generated.

I believe life to be a daily journey of worshiping God, living joyfully close in His service, and under His protection and care. These convictions are dealt with in my poetry.

I will welcome any comments.
My mailing address is:
Mrs. Wilma A. Hudgins
P.O. Box 475
Centerville, TN 37033

CONTENTS

Dedicated	v
Special Thanks	vii
Foreword	ix
Preface	xi

SECTION 1
The Wonder Of It All

A Psalm Of David	2
Nature So Bright	3
A Higher Power	4
The Wonder Of The Evening Sky	5
The Rainbow Promise	6
The Grandeur Of Creation	8
The Silvery Starlight	10
A Renewal Of Life	11
Cool, Cool Waters	12
Summer Wild Flowers	14
Fall Flowers or Fall Weeds	16
Winter Hath Come Calling	19

SECTION 2:
The Ties That Bind

Love	22
Families Are To Cherish	27
My Parents' Faith	28
My Younger Sibling	29
Sisters Together	30
What God Hath Joined Together	31
The Man Of My Dreams	32
Wedding Vows	35

He Cared For Our Children	36
In The Full Circle	37
A Curly Haired Youth	38
The Parents Of My Grandchildren	40
Grandmother's Best Wishes	42
My Husband's Birth Family	44
The Sister Of My Mother	45
In My Spiritual Kin	46
Our Brothers In Christ	47

SECTION 3
His Drawing Power

The Path Of Life	50
The People's Search	51
In His Son	52
He Is Risen Rejoice! Rejoice!	54
Worshipping Together	57
Our Preacher And His Wife	58
His Transforming Power	60
My Nephew's Family	62
My Trust In Him	64
Lord, To Thee I Pray	65

SECTION 4
A Kaleidoscope Of Splendid Folk

The Wise And Foolish Builders	68
Capable Medical Attention	69
A Name Carved On Hearts	70
College Bound	72
Pure Gold Just A' Shining	74
A Peace-Loving Man	76
A River Of Creative Dreams	78
Quoting Jesus	79

SECTION 5
After-a-While

A Few Of Heaven's "No, No's"	82
A Vision On The Wall	84
Today My Friend Went Away	85
I'll Leave On An Angel's Wing	86
Psalm 23	87

SECTION 6
A Potpourri Collection

The Prince And Princess	90
The Mother And Father Of The Bride	91
Dark, Dark Clouds With Silver Linings	92
A Modern Invention Of Around A Century Ago	94
"Hello Again"	96
The Swinging "Swang"	97
Dramatic Dreams Versus Triumphant Reality	98
A Past Time Of Life And Activity	100
My Loyal Friend	102
The Emperor's New Clothes	103

SECTION 7
Meet The Author

Wilma Armstrong Hudgins	106

SECTION 1
The Wonder Of It All

The poems in this section feature some
of the wonders of nature and the
splendors in the sky along with some
of humanities reactions to those creations.

A PSALM OF DAVID

The heavens declare the
glory of God:
The skies proclaim the work
of his hands.
Day after day they pour forth
speech;
Night after night they
display knowledge.
There is no speech or
language
Where their voice is not
heard.
Their voice goes out into all
the earth,
Their words to the ends
of the world.
In the heavens he has
pitched a tent for the sun,
Which is like a bridegroom
coming forth from his pavilion,
Like a champion rejoicing
to run his course.
It rises at one end of the
heavens
And makes its circuit to the
other;
Nothing is hidden from its
heat.
Psalm 19:1-6 (NIV)

NATURE SO BRIGHT

I saw my God today
As I sat upon a hill
And looked across
The way.
I saw Him amongst
The waving wheat.
I saw Him as the
Birds took flight
In, around, and
Through the trees,
In the soft and
Dappled light.
I saw Him in the
Winding lane, as it
Meandered through
The valley floor
And finally came
Resting at the door.
And I thank God
With all my might,
For nature so sweet,
Rare, and bright.

Genesis 1:31 (KJV) "*And God saw everything that He had made, and, behold, it was very good.*"

A HIGHER POWER

I saw my God today as I woke with a start
And searched around to see God's part in this
Day just beginning. I knew in my heart and
From experiences past that some higher power
Would begin early and stay throughout the day
Entertaining humanity in a very special way as
He presented some valuable and lasting gift
After gift. The thought gave my spirits such
An awesome thrill, joy and lift.

Through the fog there was a shimmering sun.
And while I counted each and every ray
I recognized God's gifts are never done, and on
The receiving end of each, I have won. For He
Who keeps dispensing lasting gifts, forever
Causes my spirits to soar and lift. Then the fog
Laid low to rest, and I prayed, "Thank you God
For having me as a guest, as you displayed the
Great splendors of parts of your creation."

Revelation 4:11 (NIV) "You are worthy, our Lord and God, to receive glory and honor and power, for you created all things, and by your will they were created and have their being."

THE WONDER OF THE EVENING SKY

There is often
A glorious time of day
When a large strip of the
Western sky turns crimson
And the light becomes
Dusky and irresistible.
Shortly thereafter soft
Darkness falls.

The moon glows
And the numberless stars
Wink their mysterious
Light. The wonder of the
Evening sky stands out in
A burst of glory too
Marvelous and beautiful
To describe.

Palm 19:1-4 (NCV) "The heavens declare the glory of God, and the skies announce what his hands have made."

THE RAINBOW PROMISE

I saw my God today.
The sun shown fiercely bright
And especially warm and near.
Then suddenly the clouds raced
Into view. Lightening streaked,
Thunder roared. The rain came
Slicing and slushing down.

While contemplating the dreary,
Dreamy sight, the day took on
A very shiny, rosy glow.
The atmosphere began to put
On a grand, magnificent show.
The sun careened around and
Splashed through the sky.

And then I saw it there.
A truly lofty, awesome sight,
Arousing in me such a sense
Of distinct, and special delight.

A glorious rainbow was
Stretching across and embracing
The heavens with all its might.
The magnificent colors of light
Reached as far as could be seen
With human sight.

Thanks be to our Almighty God
That with the rainbow's birth,
The promise did became ours,
That never again would water
Destroy the entire earth.

God told Noah and his sons in Genesis 9:12-15 (NIV) "This is the sign of the covenant I am making between me and you and every living creature with you, a covenant for all generations to come; I have set my rainbow in the clouds, and it will be the sign of the covenant between me and the earth. Whenever I bring clouds over the earth and the rainbow appears in the clouds, I will remember my covenant between me and you and all living creatures of every kind. Never again will the waters become a flood to destroy all life."

THE GRANDEUR OF CREATION

I saw my God today
As I gazed and thought upon life,
In its many varieties and forms,
So picturesque and intriguing in
Their various norms.

See that luscious vegetation
Reproducing so prolifically
And in such variation
As it struts, breathes. and
Lives in every nation.

Then watch the tamed pet
Animals; frolicking, playing, and
Showing their masters their
Love, as they fit into their life
Like a hand fits a glove.

And oh, those wild animals of
Intrigue, never seeming to lend
Themselves to fatigue, but running,
Roaming and scampering about in
Some direction, according to some
Route.

Not only do we treasure everything
That creeps or walks upon the land,
But also fishes and other living
Creatures in the waters and in
The seas.

Watch them flashing, flitting,
And flipping in and out of our sight
As if to tease. And see those winged
Wonders spanning across the sky,
Careening and gliding as time slips by.

Then remember there are certain keys,
Held only by God since the earth's
Foundation, to continue to unlock the
Wonder and grandeur of His marvelous
Creation.

Psalm 24:1-2 (NCV)
"The earth belongs to the Lord,
and everything in it - the world
and all it's people. He built it
on the waters and set it on the rivers."

Psalm 33:5 (KJV) "...the earth is
full of the goodness of the Lord."

THE SILVERY STARLIGHT

I saw my God today
As I reached up toward the stars so bright,
Each one filled with heaven's own light.
My reach turned to a mighty stretch,
With a yearning hand.

As my thoughts veered to a better land,
And my mind longingly lingered there,
Sweet dreams spilled in, beyond compare:
As I began to gather lustrous starlight,
With all my might, to hold it close, and
All wrapped up so secure and tight.

I wished to keep it traveling along with
Me throughout the entire starlight night
While time advanced toward morning light.
Thank you Holy God, for sparkling
Silvery starlight so bright.

Psalm 147:4-5 (NIV) "He determines the number of the stars and calls them each by name. Great is our Lord and mighty in power."

A RENEWAL OF LIFE

Spring blows right in
Heralding a renewal of life.
All over the country side
Winter's former dormant bulbs are
Popping right up through the ground
And marching across the landscape
Almost as if they are listening
To a drum and fife.

Barren winter limbs
Are suddenly exhibiting colors
And buds are appearing in clusters.
Newness permeates the very air;
Spreading beauty, joy. and wonder
Far and near all over the land
As we acclaim and celebrate again
The renewal of life.

Psalm 104:30 (NIV)
"...You renew the face of the earth."

COOL, COOL WATERS

What magic can compare to
Water on a blistering summer
Day?

Whether we jump
Into a creek or lake,
Sprint under the water hose,
Or dive off the diving board
Into the swimming pool.
It's done just to keep us cool.

But we can't resist
A little fun on the side.
So we splash, slosh, and splatter,
Causing friends and others to
Scatter.

We know they'll
Be bound to retaliate.
So we do our best to disappear
Or at the very least,
To become very scarce -
Not wanting to invite another
Water fight.

But human nature
Being just what it is:

Those whom we have
Thoroughly watered
Down, refuse to let us,
for long, hidden stay.
They manage a successful
Search for us and give the
Same measure, plus some,
Back our way.

We all push, shove, yell,
Continue hurling water, and
Generally creating a great
Fuss. 'Till one by one by
One; we begin to wear down,
And call out, "Come on!
I give - Le' me be!"

But, oh well,
Our goal was accomplished.
Our bodies became much cooler,
And we thoroughly enjoyed
A lot of fun under the sun,
In the mingled magic
Of cool water and warm weather.

✝ *GENESIS 1:7 (NCV) " So God made the air and placed some of the water above the air and some below it."*

SUMMER WILD FLOWERS

As we travel slowly
Down a winding road
A sweet perfume fills
The air.

We spy Honeysuckle
And Wild Rose vines
In the fence rows entwined.

We behold treasured fields
Of Clover blossoms
Strutting in the breeze.

Queen Anne's Lace is
Showing its lovely face
As pretty as you please.

Black Eyed Susans
Tip our way, as if to say,
 "I'll be back next year;
 I'm here to stay."

The Wonder of It All

Then the Sweet Pea vines
Wave here and there;
Knowing that summer
After summer, they'll be
Showing off their blossoms
So fair.

We see numerous other
Summer perennials:
Some familiar,
Some very rare, and,
Some perfuming up the air.

Some sport vivid colors
So clear and bright:
Red, orange, yellow, blue,
Purple, pink and white,
Giving us great delight.

And somewhere deep within,
Our thanks wells up
For such a wondrous sight
As summer's wild flowers;
So clear and bright.

✝ *Genesis 1:12 (NCV) "...Each seed grew its own kind of plant. God saw that all this was good."*

FALL FLOWERS
OR
FALL WEEDS

One person's wild weeds
Are another's wild flowers.
Autumn brings them to
Bear in such great bowers.

One sees a mass of very
Unsightly overgrown weeds
Of which this earth
Can have no possible need.
They must be destroyed
And never let go to seed.

So one gets out their mower
One fine morn, and when
Finished, the place is shorn;
Shaved clean and free
Of those offensive seeds,
Which in an unfailing way do
Yield more detested weeds.

The Wonder of It All

Another one looks at the
Same fall vegetation, and sees
Beautiful fall wild flowers;
Producing a soothing sense
Of peace and pleasure
As they grow through the sod
In old fields and pastures,
Along roadsides, in ditches,
Thickets, woodlands, waste
Areas, and along fence rows.

They come in myriads of
Gorgeous colors: brilliant
Golds, clear yellows, strong
Oranges, varied whites, soft
Pinks, pastel lilacs, dusty
Magentas, and other
Varied and glowing colors.

Those colors are sitting atop
Or alongside strong, sturdy
Green or brownish stalks,
Which are so gently flying,
Swinging, and floating
In the swaying autumn breeze.
They look very bold as they
Softly cradle the gleaming
Colorful flowers above the
Dappled leaves.

They proudly carry a variety
Of very interesting names,
Such as: Daisy Fleabone,
Ironweed, Common Thistle,
Joe-Pye, Red Sumac, Tall
Goldenrod, and Frostflowers.

You know, it matters not
Whether they are considered
Weeds or flowers; they will
Keep popping through the sod
Year after year, carrying out
The command of God.

Genesis 1:11-12 and 29 (NCV)
"Then God said, 'Let the earth produce
plants – some to make grain for seeds
and others to make fruits with seed in them.
Every seed will produce more of its
own kind of plant.' And it happened.
The earth produced plants with grain for seeds
and trees that made fruits with seeds in them.
each seed grew its own kind of plant.
God saw that all this was good."

God said, 'Look, I have given you
all the plants that have grain for seeds
and all the trees whose fruits have seeds
in them. They will be food for you."

WINTER HATH COME CALLING

Winter hath come calling, bold and cold.
And as the North wind doth howl and blow,
Often times it gives to us quite a show.
Freezing temperatures bring lustrous ice.
The sparkle, glitter and splendor doth entice
Us to bundle up tight, both young and old,
Then go out and challenge the ice and cold.

And if the children's hopes do win out,
There'll be crystal snow flying all about,
Tantalizing us to build snow men and to
Find places to slip, glide, skate, and slide.
Never mind the rosy cheeks, purple lips,
And red nose, along with the semi frozen
Fingers, bent ears, and the turned up toes.

It's just a testimony to what may happen
When winter hath come calling and the
North wind doth again howl and blow!

Psalm 74:17 (NIV)) "It was you who set all the boundaries of the earth; you made both summer and winter."

SECTION 2:

The Ties That Bind

The members of a family make
up the most enduring ties on earth.
God Himself created the very first
family unit, as recorded in Genesis
chapter two. I tried in these poems
to celebrate the spirit of this special
bond which exists between individual
family members.

LOVE

Love is patient,
Love is kind.
It does not envy,
It does not boast,
It is not proud,
It is not rude,
It is not self-seeking,
It is not easily angered,
It keeps no record of wrongs.
Love does not delight in evil
But rejoices with the truth.
It always protects,
Always trusts,
Always hopes,
Always perseveres.

Quoted from I Corinthians
13:4-7 (NIV)

AN ARMSTRONG FAMILY PICTURE

Children, along with their spouses, of Lanty and Emma Armstrong

1970

A WILMA AND CLARA FAMILY PICTURE

Wilma Hudgins and Clara Shannon are daughters of Sid and Arlis Armstrong. The picture is all the immediate members of Wilma and Clara's families in 1994.

The Ties That Bind

A HUDGINS' FAMILY PICTURE

Thirteen of the sixteen children born to
Ollie and Annie Lou Hudgins.
1990'S

I Saw My God Today While Walking The Path Of Life

WEDDING PICTURE OF

Wilma and Wayne Hudgins
July 3, 1956

FAMILIES ARE TO CHERISH

Having a family
Is like owning a jewel rare,
To which nothing else can compare.
There is something about a family gene
Which causes us on each other to lean.
We recognize each call and need.
And it is love that prompts us
That call to heed.

The word "family" is a special name:
One of very sweet and most precious fame.
The human tongue loves that word to frame;
And often uses it, the human heart to tame.
Even the thoughts of family
Will often bring down cherished showers
Of blessings, like softly falling rain.

And so my treasured family
With your affectionate devotion
And beautiful charm, you bring delight
To my life. And it feels so right!
You add such enrichment sweet;
Encased in a splendor and beauty so neat!
"Dear precious and priceless family,
I do love you so!"

*I John 4:7 (NIV) " ...let us love one another,
for love comes from God."*

MY PARENTS' FAITH

I saw my God today,
As my Dad spoke of people
Being righteous and good,
And how everyone should
Live as best they could.

And when I saw my Mother
In her usual place, studying
Her Bible, and when finished,
Marking the page with an
Old piece of lovely lace;

I began to thank God for my
Privilege rare, of having wise
Loving parents to enfold me
In their special care.

Deuteronomy 6:5-7 (NIV)
"Love the Lord your God
with all your heart
and with all your soul
and with all your strength.
These commandments that I
give you today are to be upon
your heart."

MY YOUNGER SIBLING

I saw my God today
In my little sibling's
Priceless innocence.
My life is filled with joy,
Happiness and delight.
My spirit is elevated
To a greater height.

As I reflect upon my
Sweet-hearted little
Sister sent from above,
She fills my existence
With a special love.
She adores me without
Censor or reservation,
Causing me to catch a
Glimpse of the Lord's
Grand salvation.

And, I thank you, my
Lord God, for this little
Sibling sublime and
That you allow me to
Call her mine.

*In Matthew 19:14 (NCV) Jesus said,
"Let the little children come to me."*

SISTERS TOGETHER

My sister has a character so divine,
And a beauty of spirit so sublime.
In goodness and strength, few others
Compare.

When I need her, she's always there.
She is my friend in times of inspiration
Or despair.

We giggle together, we love together.
We weep together, we pray together.
We worship together, we study together.
We care and we share together.

You see we sisters share a special bond
Designed to enjoy a close togetherness.
And so sister, my sister dear,
Forever I shall hold you very tightly,
Deep down inside of this my heart;
And there together shall we ever be
As treasures you continue to impart!

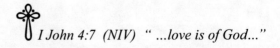
I John 4:7 (NIV) " ...love is of God..."

WHAT GOD HATH JOINED TOGETHER

I saw my God today
While enjoying the benefits
Of being married to a fine
Christian man.

When he calls me his queen
And invites me on him to lean;
When he pulls me close to his
Side, declaring his love will
Forever abide; when he says
I am the pleasure of his life,
And he is so proud to call me
His wife; I then realize what
A treasure I have in this man;

And I again thank God for his
Great proclamation that a man
Should cleave unto his wife
And they would become one
Body.

Genesis 2:23 (NIV) The man said. "This is now bone of my bones and flesh of my flesh; she shall be called 'woman', because she was taken out of man."

THE MAN OF MY DREAMS

Before we married, I dreamed about
A very special man. At first I didn't
Recognize you. But now after these
Years of marriage the stuff that
Dreams are made of is reaching me
Loud and clear. Your everyday
Actions express such kindness, love,
And thoughtfulness: The real stuff
That dreams are made of!

You open the car door for me in the
Midst of a gushy rain - what a sight -
As well as when the sun is shining
Down very clear and bright.

You frequently throw a
Very protective arm around me
As though to shield and save me
From any and all pain.

You say, "What can I do to help
You, Honey?" when we are about
To entertain, even though later you
May wonder why you said such
A thing!

The Ties That Bind

I treasure the glint of satisfaction
To be read in your eye
When you make a special effort
To introduce me to some guy.

I feel so safe when I see that glint
Of steel in your eye if you think
That someone or some thing might
Dare to harm or dishonor my life.

You are my very special companion.
You have kept me from the bleak
Embrace of loneliness and filled
My life with warmth and laughter.

When you compliment my
Looks, my mind, my disposition,
Or my individualistic spirit,
You bring me such sweet joy.

When you love our children and
Help me as we strive to bring them up
In the nurture and admonition of the Lord,
Our hearts sing together in one accord.

I Saw My God Today While Walking The Path Of Life

Because of your spirituality, we have
Together glimpsed the gates of heaven and
The home of the soul awaiting us there,
Which we hope and pray to share.

When you look at me with eyes of pride
And say, "This is my wife," you give
Such golden meaning to my life, and
I know we are one in the bond of love.

When storms of life swirl around me,
And you hold me close and invite me
Into your loving care until the storm passes,
Then I know I am blessed beyond compare.

Your spiritual leadership and companionship
As we pray together and play together
Nourishes my soul as we travel through
This life and toward that land beyond.

All these things and others too numerous
To mention, make you my dream man,
Forever special in my sight.
And so I honor you with all my might.

Ephesians 5:33 (NIV) "...each one of you must love his wife as he loves himself, and the wife must respect her husband."

WEDDING VOWS
RUTH 1:16-17 (KJV)

"Entreat me not to leave thee,
or to return from following after thee:
for whither thou goest, I will go;
and where thou lodgest, I will lodge:
thy people shall be my people,
and thy God my God:
Where thou diest, will I die,
And there will I be buried:
The Lord do so to me, and more also,
If ought but death part thee and me."

(Note: Several years ago the above words from the Book of Ruth, taken from the King James version of the Holy Bible, were sometimes used by the bride in repeating her wedding vows. This was true in the wedding of "The Dream Man" and his young bride, Wilma.)

HE CARED FOR OUR CHILDREN

I saw my God today,
As I watched our children wrestle and play;
With each other, with friends, with the dogs,
With the cats and with other lively kin.

As I watched them narrowly escaping
Various bruises and injuries,
I thought of how God was holding them
In the hollow of His hand.

And I prayed,
"Oh, God, please keep them there,
Until the girls become women,
And each of the boys becomes a man."

"And then please help them
To live out their lives
The very best that they can,
And all according to your plan.

Matthew 19:14 (NIV) "Let the little children come to me, and do not hinder them, for the Kingdom of Heaven belongs to such as these."

IN THE FULL CIRCLE

Not so long ago
A little tow-head
Called out in the night,
"Mommy, it's dark and
I cannot see the light."

And I said,
"Hold my hand, Darling.
Mommy will keep you safe
In the night."

So with his little hand
Tucked away in mine,
He walked strong and secure
Through the darkness
Into the light.

Tonight, a gray-haired woman
Called out, "Son, it's dark
And I cannot see the light."

A strong young man said,
"Mom, hold my hand.
I'll keep you safe
And bring you to the light.
And so I tucked my hand
Away in his,
And with firm, sure steps
He led me safe,
Out of the darkness,
Into the light.

And so we have come
Full circle, my Son!
And I thank God
For you, my Son!

✠ *Proverbs 4:3 (KJV) "...I was my father's son, tender and only beloved in the sight of my mother."*

A CURLY HAIRED YOUTH

Curly haired youth, handsome and tall
Some day a man answering life's call.

He came into this world bright eyed
And quick. He captured our hearts.
Made us laugh! Made us tick!

The Ties That Bind

Entered school, all bubbly and bright;
Learned quickly, made friends easily;
Saw some good times
And some times gave us fright.

The years came and went;
Clicking away! Clicking away!
He was always in the mother's heart
Buried deep, and there to stay!

Only mothers throughout time,
Only God of all the ages,
Comprehends and understands
Mother's bonds through all the stages.

Dear Father's – quiet though they be –
Support, correct and befriend.
And they want all the world to see
This is my Son, and he takes after me.

Handsome son, as we love you today,
Use your talents, guard your strength,
Seek your wisdom from above,
And always savor your parents' love.

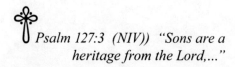
Psalm 127:3 (NIV)) "Sons are a heritage from the Lord,..."

THE PARENTS OF MY GRANDCHILDREN

Parents! Dear great parents!
How they love you!
You welcomed them when
They were brand-new.
You wrap them up tight in your
Arms. You shield and defend
Them from harm.

Your eyes glow when on
Your shoulders they ride.
Often you rock them, or
Hold them upside down, or
Bounce them on your knees,
Until thy cry out "Do it again,
Please, please!"

You work for them from
Daylight 'till dark. But still
Take time to leave upon them
Your mark of honesty, joy
Gentleness, and laughter,
Peace, honor, temperance,
And hard work. And you
Teach them never from their
Duty to shirk.

You convince each little
Daughter that she is a
Princess so beautiful and fair.
And your son knows he is
Special and loved. He knows
That he and his Dad make a pair;
That he's Daddy's little man,
Strong and smart.

You praise my grandchildren.
You play and pray with them.
You attend games, school events,
Recitals, awards ceremonies,
Sports functions. and on and on
We could go but, oh well, the rest
You know. Some day they'll
Leave the nest; and then as on
Life's ventures they embark,
You'll be a special treasure
Buried deep inside their hearts -
Forever more - until they reach
That eternal shore! Thanks to
Our God, for you dear parents!

Ephesians 6:4 (KJV) "...fathers, provoke not your children to wrath: but bring them up in the nurture and admonition of the Lord."

GRANDMOTHER'S BEST WISHES

Turning twenty-one is a
Very special milestone.
I pray you will never
Need to be alone.
I trust you will always
Have showers of love.

You are so dear to so many.
Do you not clearly see?
All your days you have been
Taught much truth. And as
You know, it is the truth that
Sets you free!

At twenty-one you are dealing
With life-time decisions. If you
Keep God first, under all kinds
Of conditions, it will help, as
You pursue your very special
Ambitions!

For you, we are so very
Grateful and so very proud!

You have resisted illegal
Drugs and many other tragic
Evils: Putting to flight
Treacherous and enticing
Attractions.

May God keep you in His
Love and in His care: Helping
You with burdens you will
Sometimes need to bear:
And rejoicing with you as His
Son's name you wear.

Then may you travel that
Narrow road so rare, until you
Reach that heavenly home
Which for us He did prepare,
And to which none other can
Compare.

II Timothy 1:5 (KJV) "...I call to remembrance the...unfeigned faith that is in thee, which dwelt first in thy grandmother ...and thy mother... and I am persuaded in thee also."

MY HUSBAND'S BIRTH FAMILY

Only one birth sibling I had
To treasure and to love.
So when my marriage presented me
With twenty-seven in-law-siblings,
It was a time to be glad.

They have been such a pleasure.
Once I became their brother's wife
They accepted me into their heart
And life.

They have kept me there!
Many occasions we all do share;
As we continue to love the same dear
Man.

Thank you, gracious God
For my husband and his birth family.
Please keep us together and in your
Care.

I John 4:7 (NIV)
"Love comes from God."

THE SISTER OF MY MOTHER

You are the sister of my mother. Therefore,
You occupy a place in my heart that cannot
Be given to any other.

As my memories wander, through them
I can see how you've been so beautiful
And such a blessing to me!

As a child, with happiness, I looked up to you.
And to my childish needs you were always true.

The years flew by. We each found our God.
We each found our mates. We played with our
Children.

We shared many joys. We shared some sorrows.
We developed a friendship to carry throughout
 All tomorrows.

And so I feel a need for prayer, to express my
Thankfulness for the love I share with my aunt,
Who is my dear mother's sister.

*Philippians 1:3 (KJV) "I thank my
God upon every remembrance of you,..."*

IN MY SPIRITUAL KIN

I saw my God today, as I interacted with my
Spiritual kin. Dear brother of mine, dear sister of
Mine, upon every remembrance of your kindness;
Upon every thought of your loving care; through
Christ who made us new, I thank our God for you.

I thank Him for your words of comfort, when
Deep troubles darken my day. I thank Him for
Your encouragement when Satan hurls temptations
My way. I thank Him for our laughter as we tease,
As we converse, and as we play. I thank Him for
Your gentle graciousness, which means more than
I could ever say.

I thank our God you share a pew with me as we
Admonish one another in hymns and spiritual songs.
I'm thankful to our God that with one accord we
Pray, commune, give, and listen, with joy in our
Hearts, as we worship our Lord. Praise be to our
God for spiritual relatives so near and so dear!

*John 13:35 (NCV) "All people will know
that you are my followers if you love each other."*

OUR BROTHERS IN CHRIST

Dear brothers in Christ.
You are so special and meet our needs so exactly:
How could we ever get along without you?
With your nobility of character and the
Strength God has given to you Christian brethren
To draw the line concerning matters divine;
And to stand firmly for what you know is right;
Your stability brings to us such great delight.

God commissioned men to love their wives
And to bring their children up in the nurture
And admonition of the Lord. How necessary
That love and guidance is to the well being
Of the family unit. Thank you God.

When during church services you men lead
Us in fervent prayers, inspirational songs, and
Fill our pulpits with righteous exhortations and
Encouragements: we begin to understand and
To comprehend some of the evidence of God's
Wisdom as He empowered our men to fulfill
Such basic and spiritual needs.

Romans 10:15 (KJV) "...How beautiful are the feet of them that preach the gospel of peace and bring glad tidings of good things!"

SECTION 3
His Drawing Power

Our Lord has such extraordinary
drawing power that it causes us
to freely and frequently worship
Him in praise and in prayer.

THE PATH OF LIFE

I saw my God today
As I strode amidst the path of life.

I saw Him as His people were
Walking tall and refusing small.
I saw Him in the babies' ready smiles,
As I gazed upon them for awhile.
I saw Him in the old and knarred hands
Of ones who have served as best they can.
I saw Him in the young and brave
As they determined to conquer Earth,
Space and the grave.
I saw Him in the steadfastness of the
Mid-aged as they wadded through
Their dreams; and went about making
Hand-prints in the bulwarks of time.

And I give thanks to my God above
For humanities versatile shine:
A true kaleidoscope divine.

"I Corinthians (NCV) "There are different kinds of service, but the same Lord."

THE PEOPLE'S SEARCH

I saw my God today.
I saw Him in the people's search
As they filed into the country
Church.

I saw Him as they worshipped
There, sending songs, sermons,
And gifts wafting upward along
With fervent prayer.

I heard Him in the preacher's
Voice as he spoke of the Christ
And ask listeners to make their
Choice.

And I thank my God today for
The Son that He gave, for the pain
That He bore, and because He is
Mine forevermore.

John 4:24 (NIV) "God is spirit, and His worshipers must worship in spirit and in truth."

IN HIS SON

I saw my God today
In His Son:

While leaning on His strength
And trusting in His power;

While exploring His earthly life
And glorying in His light;

While praying through His name
And singing His praises;

While continuing in His word
And submitting to His rule;

While accepting His cleansing
and receiving His grace;

While following His counsel
And walking in His way;

While glorying in His truth
And basking in His freedom;

While knocking at His door
And receiving His welcome;

And – while living life more
Abundantly.

His Drawing Power

I saw my God today in the
Followers of His Son:

As they lived lives of faith
   And walked in the Spirit;

As they grew in knowledge
   And resisted temptation;

As they showed patience
   And became kind and gentle;

As they prayed for
   And then extended forgiveness;

As they valued righteousness
   And practiced obedience;

And as they were
   Grounded in truth and love.

What a vision of pure delight
   To see our Father God;
   Through His Son,
   Jesus the Christ!

Jesus said in John 14:9 (NIV) "Anyone who has seen me has seen the Father."

HE IS RISEN
REJOICE! REJOICE!

Upon a memorable day Jesus triumphantly entered
Jerusalem. He was followed by many, loudly crying,
"Hosanna! Blessed is He who comes in the name of
The Lord!"

Then dark Friday invaded that week - bringing with
It cruelty, anguish and pain beyond belief as the cry
Now turned to shouts of, "Crucify Him! Crucify Him!"

They plaited a crown of thorns and placed it on His
Head. He went through the outrage of being scourged-
Leaving his body ripped, bruised, and bleeding.

He carried His own cross till he fell beneath the load.
Then another came to his aid and carried it on up the
Hill to Golgotha.

There, the nails were hammered into His hands
Attaching Him to that cross of pain and bitter shame.
They abused Him, and they hurled insults at Him.

Instead of calling down angels to save Him, he said,
"Father, forgive them for they know not what they do!"
Then He cried in a loud voice and gave up His spirit.

With a sword they pierced His side. Both blood and
Water poured out deep and wide, indicating a heart
Broken inside. The earth shook. Its creator had died.

The rocks split. Many tombs opened. The curtain
In the temple was torn in twain. The sun stopped
Shining, and darkness came over the land.

On this earth He had no where to lay his head. In
Death he was placed in a rich man's new tomb, hewn
Out of rock. The tomb was secured and guards posted.

On that dark Friday, His disciples were frightened,
Saddened, disillusioned, and distraught. Somehow
They made it through the Sabbath.

Early Sunday morning found some of the women at
The tomb. An angel ask them, "Why do you seek the
Living among the dead? He is not here. He has risen."

They were startled and frightened, yet filled with great
Joy. They went immediately to spread the glad tidings
To His other disciples; "Our Lord has risen." Rejoice!

Soon Jesus met with the others; explaining that all
Power had been given to Him in heaven and on earth;
Telling them to go into all the world and make disciples.

So go they did! Now, some two thousand years later,
Christians do celebrate His resurrection. Our Lord
Has risen from the dead! Rejoice! Let our voices ring!

Our Jesus, who conquered death, is now our leader
And our king. Grant that I may follow Him all the way
Through death, into Heaven, and with the Angels sing,
"Hosanna! Blessed be the name of the Lord!"

*Luke 24:5 (NIV) "Why do you look
for the living among the dead?
He is not here, he has risen!"*

WORSHIPPING TOGETHER

Dear loved one, acquaintance,
Complete stranger or friend:
By meeting with our spiritual
Family and sharing in our
Worship service on this very
Special day, you have spread
Many a sunshine ray.

You have added to our joy
More than we could ever say.
May your soul be exhaulted, and
Your heart be filled with cheer.
May the time for us to again
Share worship - be very near.
Until then, may the Lord
Bless and keep us all under
His care and in His service.

Psalm 95:6 (NIV) "Come, let's worship Him and bow down. Let's kneel before the Lord who made us because he is our God."

OUR PREACHER AND HIS WIFE

I do want to honor you
With sincere words; some that
Will be heard with your listening
Heart.

And with this task I hardly know
Where to start. But this you must
Know: that you have caused
Myself and numerous others to
Love you so!

There truly is no language upon
This great earth which can possibly
Express the untold worth of a
Faithful gospel preacher and his
Noble wife, who gives needed
Support – lives, loves, and labors by
His side.

You have gained
Much admiration and respect:
Yes, even allegiance

As you have busied yourselves
With good works,
And a great dedication to God,
And to His word.

His Drawing Power

You have devotedly, eloquently,
And effectively taught truth;
Enlightened us and refuted error.
Your efforts, to reach each and
Every member of the congregation
In very meaningful and joyous
Ways, has not gone unnoticed
And will be forever praised.
Your work in the community
Is greatly appreciated and to be
Highly commended.

May God continue to richly bless
You and keep us together for many
Years upon this earth, as you continue
To help us in our preparations to enjoy
Eternity with the saved of all the ages
And to forever live in the presence of
Our God and of each other.

II Timothy 4:2 (NIV) "Preach the Word; be prepared in season an out of season, correct, rebuke and encourage – with great patience and careful instruction."

HIS TRANSFORMING POWER

Today
I ran into a friend from days gone by-
One for whom I had often prayed
And breathed many a fearful sigh:

Through the years I had observed
That he was staid on questioning
Whether there could be a God,
All the while refusing
To let Him come anywhere nigh.

As my friend and I chatted,
I observed attitudes so very new.
His life had found a blessed cure
And was now shining and pure.

He no longer was questioning God,
But rather, he was rejoicing in Him.
His anger had changed to kindness.
Hate had changed to powerful love.
Now he was busy thanking his God
For blessings from above.

I knew this great and blessed
Change in my friend had been
Wrought in the furnace of life:
As he had invited Christ to
Give to him a tower of strength
To mold and reshape his thoughts,
Minute by minute, hour by hour;
According to God's
Transcending, transforming power!

He had asked for strength
To live his life day by day,
In such a grand victorious way,
That now he continues to say,
God gave to me His Christ;
And that has changed my life.

✞ Romans 12:2 (NCV) "Do not be shaped by this world; instead be changed from within by a new way of thinking. Then you will be able to decide what God wants for you; you will know what is good and pleasing to him and what is perfect."

MY NEPHEW'S FAMILY

Wow! What a Nephew!
When I think of my sister's son I
Remember that when a youngster,
He and his friends were always
In the midst of some kind of stir.
Usually involving a lot of laughter,
Action, teasing and fun. They
Were good kids, and many a
Neighbor's confidence they
Won!

Wow! What a Family!
Eventually David met a dear,
Sweet and lovely young woman.
His heart she did quickly capture.
Marriage closely followed. They
Soon found their mission in life.
He became a full-time preacher:
Making her the preacher's wife.

Soon their number became five.
They are now raising three
Children fair - who have learned
From their parents to deal with a
Lot of laughter and fun, while at
The same time being filled with
Care for others as they minister
To many varying religious, social,
And individual needs.

As a family they have served in
Several American states and in
Some other countries as well.
Wherever they go they have
Built a reputation of being a rich
Blessing to those around them.

May they forever be in God's
Service. May they be nourished
And cherished with His loving and
Abundant care: this in answer to
Many a fervent prayer!

I Corinthians 1:3 (NIV) "Grace and peace to you from God our Father and the Lord Jesus Christ."

MY TRUST IN HIM

I've been so blessed
My whole life through
Because I was taught,
My Lord, to trust in you.

Making life's decisions
Demands much trust
In thee Lord Almighty
Whose judgment is just.

As life makes its mark:
And I pursue my quest;
Trusting in You, Lord,
I can find sweet rest.

Yes, trusting my Lord,
Insures unparalleled
Reward. Thank you
Blessed Lord.

 Psalm 2:12 (KJV)"...Blessed are all they that put their trust in Him."

LORD, TO THEE I PRAY

Lord grant to me another day:
To live a lot, to love a lot, to give a lot,
To pray a lot, to help a lot, to think a lot,
To work a lot, to see a lot, to smile a lot,
And to dream a lot.

But if today will be my last:
Cleanse me, and hug me so very tight
Until this life is in the past.
Then take me home to your celestial light,
To live in peace and holy delight!

* Philippians 4:6-7 (NIV)) "Do not be anxious about anything, but in everything, by prayer and petition, with thanksgiving, present your requests to God. And the peace of God, which transcends all understanding, will guard your hearts and your minds in Christ Jesus."*

SECTION 4

A Kaleidoscope Of Splendid Folk

Kaleidoscopes are made up of numerous shapes and colors in various combinations to make very different and unique designs; bringing beauty and joy to the observer.

Humanity in its many differences provides the viewer with an unending kaleidoscopic view of much human strength, honor, talent, and beauty. There are rare and numerous differing ways to serve the Lord and we are each endowed with the ability to set goals and to accomplish different objectives.

THE WISE AND FOOLISH BUILDERS

"Therefore everyone who hears these words of mine and puts them into practice is like a wise man who built his house on the rock. The rain came down, the streams rose, and the winds blew and beat against that house: yet it did not fall, because it had its foundation on the rock. But everyone who hears these words of mine and does not put them into practice is like a foolish man who built his house on sand. The rain came down, the streams rose, and the winds blew and beat against that house, and it fell with a great crash."

Matthew 7:24-27 (NIV)

(Note: When composing the poems in this section concerning "splendid folk" I was reminded of Jesus words about the wise and foolish builders as quoted above.)

CAPABLE MEDICAL ATTENTION

Today I wrestled with
A bodily affliction.
The kind that leaves you
Scared, questioning.
Wondering why, and
What now?

Then I saw God's deep
Abiding care, in the
Skill of my physician,
Who kindly assessed
The situation and with
God there, made the
Right decision.

How thankful I am for
Nurturing, sustaining,
And capable medical
Attention.

I now give my God
Thanks and praise for
Special help and care
Throughout my days.

I Peter 5:7 (NIV) "Cast all your anxiety on him because he cares for you."

A NAME CARVED ON HEARTS

After she was gone
Someone carved her name on granite.

While here below
Beginning with the celebration of her birth
She carved her name on hearts.

Mom and Dad praised her.
Siblings acknowledged her worth.
She was such an inspiration on this earth.

Her husband and children
Loved, honored and adored her.
They all rose up and called her blessed.

Co-workers gained strength from
Her friendliness, kindness, and wisdom,
Along with her cooperative spirit.

Neighbors looked forward to her help and
Attention, which she spread all around her
With love, warmth, and affection.

Brothers and sisters in the church loved
And respected her strength, humility,
And dedication to them and to her God.

She could just walk into a room, smile,
And cause hearts to glow in the warmth of
Her strong, gentle, and caring presence.

She truly was a treasured jewel, who
Demonstrated her faith through actions
As she busied herself serving others. No
Wonder her name is carved on many a
Heart.

Proverbs 31:25-31 (NCV)) "She is strong and is respected by the people. She looks forward to the future with joy. She speaks wise words, and teaches others to be kind. She watches over her family and never wastes her time. Her children speak well of her. Her husband also praises her, saying, 'There are many fine women but you are better than all of them.' Charm can fool you, and beauty can trick you, but a woman who respects the Lord should be praised. Give her the reward she has earned: She should be praised in public for what she has done."

COLLEGE BOUND

Our little girl is
Leaving for college today.
There was so much more
We had wanted to teach her:
So many more things
We had wanted to say.
But she's on her way:
College bound this very day.

It seems but yesterday
We brought her home to stay.
The thought of her ever leaving
Seemed so very far away.
We had such high hopes,
Such dreams, such plans,
And each brother took care of
Her like a little man.

We tried so hard
To show her the true way.
It wasn't always easy:
We often knelt to pray.
But thanks be to God,
Goodness had it's way
And now obviously plans to stay.

Someone told us just the other day,
"Your daughter has grown into
Such a lovely young lady. She's so
Beautiful within and without." Our
Hearts wanted to shout, "Yes, and
She spreads that beauty all about."

We've watched her grow loving,
Strong, patient, and kind. Her heart
Always ready to reach out with a
Helping hand whether it be for a
Loved one, a friend, a camp, a class,
A child, or wherever she can.

Dear Lord, we'll painfully miss her.
The foot of our bed will seem so
Empty when she isn't sitting there to
Talk with us late into the night:
The girl talk, her sense of humor,
And her winning ways.

Dear God, our Father, please keep her
Safe on this journey which is taking
Her away into uncharted paths. Give
Life to the thoughts that through your
Word have been sown; never, ever
Leave her alone! She is our precious
Daughter, and we do love her so!

Ecclesiastes 12:1 (NIV) "Remember your creator in the days of your youth."

PURE GOLD
JUST A' SHINING

Gold is a very precious metal.
I like the word "golden"
When speaking of older citizens.
It's saying that age holds,
And yet dispenses much
Very useful and special treasure,
Treasure that is like pure gold,
Just a' shining.

Age many times smoothes out
The uneven edges and brings
"A diamond out of the rough."
The experience of aging
Often brings rare wisdom,
Like pure gold, just a' shining.

Age sometimes sees beauty and
A use for all that accumulated stuff.
Age will even approve
Of the talent and exuberance of
Untamed youth - which is
Like pure gold, just a' shining.

Age understands the blessings
In hard work, hard knocks,
And hard sacrifices to
Alleviate the hard needs of others.
This understanding born of age
Is like pure gold, just a' shining.

Age has dealt with happiness,
Joy, and laughter: as it has
Traveled across this stage called
Life. So it leaves a message
For future sojourners,
Like pure gold, just a' shining.

Especially important are
"Golden Age Banquets."
Young folks work hard and
Prepare for a special people whom
They treasure and wish to honor -
Like pure gold, just a' shining.

(Note: I once heard a story about a younger woman becoming very impressed with the patience, kindness, courtesy, and love of an older woman of her acquaintance. The young one remarked, "I'd give my life to become such a woman." The older one, in her wisdom, replied, "That's just what it has cost me, young lady.")

Proverbs 16:31 (NCV) "Gray hair is like a crown of honor. It is earned by living a good life."

A PEACE-LOVING MAN

He wished everyone
Would practice peace.

He realized –
As the old saying goes,
"That would be a little bit
Of heaven on earth."

Upon contemplation
He knew that he could
Control only one person:
That one being himself.

When a difference
Of opinion arose
Between him and his
Family, friends, neighbors,
Or acquaintances,
He made every effort to fix
It, before the sun went down.

He began to live his life
Every day so that he made
Very faithful friends
All along the way.

If he saw friction a' brewing,
He learned how to
Pour the oil of kindness
And forgiveness
On troubled waters.

He became a true and
Stalwart gentleman
Who refused to stir up strife.
So peace reigned supreme
In his life. And what
A wonderfully blest life
It turned out to be!

☦ *Romans 14:19 (KJV) "Let us therefore follow after the things which make for peace,..."*

Matthew 5:9 (KJV) "Blessed are the peacemakers: for they shall be called the children of God."

Colossians 3:15 (KJV) "... let the peace of God rule in your hearts,..."

A RIVER OF CREATIVE DREAMS

Today I read an article in the local newspaper:
One showing how the human spirit often shines
While sailing down a river of creative dreams
And believing that imagination and dedication,
Provide the means for accomplishing feats
That improve and make things a whole lot better
When those in a group happily cooperate and
Work together.

Thank you God for giving to your human beings
The ability, desire, and strength to grow and
Provide the light that makes progress in attaining
Dreams just right, before it is night. May God bless
The efforts of all civic groups who are intent upon
Devising, setting in motion, and implementing
Individual and community improvements.

I Corinthians 12:5 (NCV)
"There are different ways to serve..."

QUOTING JESUS

After this manner
Therefore pray ye:
Our Father
Which art in heaven,
Hallowed be Thy name,

Thy kingdom come.
Thy will be done
In earth,
As it is in heaven.

Give us this day
Our daily bread.

And forgive us our debts,
As we forgive our debtors.

And lead us not
Into temptation,
But deliver us from evil:
For thine is the kingdom,
And the power, and the glory,
For ever.
Amen.

Matthew 6:9-13 (KJV)

SECTION 5
After-a-While

Since the beginning of time humanity has had a fascination with – and a deep longing for – life after death. The poems in this section deal with this subject matter and scripture references are used as validation.

A FEW OF HEAVEN'S "NO, NO'S"

No searching
For the medicine cabinet:
It will not be a necessity.
There'll be no illness there,
For such is heaven's destiny.

Wipe out that fear of death,
Tears, sorrow, and crying.
For in heaven, there will be
No need for sighing!

Happiness, joy, and delight,
Along with bliss and laughter,
Will surely engulf us in that
Eternal ever after.

No night will be there.
So don't expect to flip on a light.
God's glory will be shining
Brighter than the sun is bright.

Door keys will not be needed in
Heaven. God is its center.
There will be no need for locks,
Because painful sin cannot enter.

After-a-While

There'll be no need for worry in
That life. There'll be nothing about
Which to fret. There'll be no one
To stir up strife.

There'll be no thieves, murderers,
Rapists, terrorists, or liars.
There'll be people living
Lives that are pure and right.

No temples or church buildings
Will be seen; For Heaven's
Temple is Jesus, the Lamb, and
His Father, the King.

Won't it be wonderful on that
Heavenly shore, mingling with the
Saved of all the ages, and enjoying
God's presence forever more.

Revelation 21:22 (NIV)
"I did not see a temple in the city,
because the Lord God Almighty and
the Lamb are its temple."

A VISION ON THE WALL

They were singing a sweet,
Sweet song of salvation. What
A delight! To her heart it brought
Great elation. She looked up and
Saw a departed loved one in a
Fantasy vision on the wall. He was
Striding toward her, so handsome,
Ageless, and tall, leading thousands
Through beautiful flowers and
Pastures green.

Their faces were filled with
Happiness and looking so serene.
As she very hungrily and intensely
Gazed, the vision did disappear:
Leaving her amazed. But she was
Beautifully reminded that she had
Nothing to fear, while her own
Eternal departure was growing more
And more near: And the blessed time
For reunion was growing more and
More dear.

Revelation 21:4 (NCV)
"... there will be no more death, sadness,
crying, or pain, because all the old ways
are gone."

After-a-While

TODAY MY FRIEND WENT AWAY

My friend left me today.
In that hearse they rolled him away,
Down to the grave, where he would lay.

But I still have my memories bright,
Of those special childish times of delight,
When we romped and played in each other's sight.

And then as traveling time refused to stay,
We journeyed our separate ways.
But we never forgot those earlier days.

When occasionally as adults we saw each other,
We reminisced as if we were sister and brother.
And we reclaimed our nearness one to the other.

Then as time turned into years;
Individually we experienced laughter and tears,
But we never gave way to abject fears.

Because early in life we gave ourselves
To our Lord - now we still are bound by that cord.
So, dear friend, I'll see you on the other side!

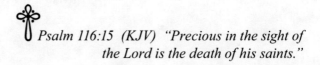

Psalm 116:15 (KJV) "Precious in the sight of the Lord is the death of his saints."

I'LL LEAVE ON AN ANGEL'S WING

Some day I'll leave on an angel's wing.
Cry for me some but not too much!
Just let me go because I love you so.
And where I'm going you know.

We've often spoken of it so many times
Here below. It's what we've lived for
Our whole life through: to inhabit an
Immortal body, all new!

We wondered who would first go.
Now my time is so very near.
So without doubts and fear, let it be so.
Don't long to keep me here.

Rejoice with me as my flight draws nigh
To fly through and beyond the sky,
To our beautiful eternal home on high.
Then bid me God-speed
As I leave on an Angel's wing.

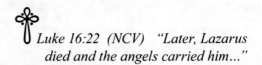

Luke 16:22 (NCV) *"Later, Lazarus died and the angels carried him..."*

PSALM 23

"The Lord is my shepherd, I
shall not be in want.
He makes me lie down in
green pastures,
he leads me beside quiet waters,
he restores my soul.
He guides me in paths of
righteousness
for his name's sake.
Even though I walk through the
Valley of the shadow of death,
I will fear no evil,
for you are with me:
your rod and your staff,
they comfort me.
You prepare a table before me
in the presence of my enemies.
You anoint my head with oil;
my cup overflows.
Surely goodness and love will
follow me all the days of my life,
and I will dwell in the house
of the Lord forever.

(NIV)

SECTION 6
A Potpourri Collection

When thinking of potpourri we usually think of a mixture of dried flower petals and spices kept in some kind of neat container for the purpose of enjoying their fragrance. In this instance we are calling a collection of miscellaneous poems a potpourri collection.

THE PRINCE AND PRINCESS

Dearest Rebecca our Princess rare.
Found her Prince beyond compare.

Charles so handsome – mind, body and soul:
Captured her heart, – so special to behold.

The day has arrived. It's all been arranged.
The two will be one – precious vows exchanged.

May God richly bless this wonderful pair
As life's entwinement they forever share!

(Note: This couple is now raising three
beautiful young daughters, all of whom are
little China dolls – their parents having
adopted them from the country of China.)

Hebrews 13:4 (NCV) "Marriage should be honored by everyone, and husband and wife should keep their marriage pure."

THE MOTHER AND FATHER OF THE BRIDE

TO THE MOTHER:
Dear tired mother of the bride,
Your daughter has temporarily
Flown from your side.
But soon she'll return
With hubby so sweet.
The family they will raise
Will be quite a treat.
And once again your life
Will be joyfully complete.

TO THE DAD:
Dear dad, you've been so
Patient and kind, hard work
Seeming never to mind.
After the wedding you said,
"I'm through," but we know
You'll find ways to give to the
New family too, as you continue
Nourishing and cherishing them
Your whole life through.

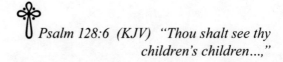

Psalm 128:6 (KJV) "Thou shalt see thy children's children...,"

DARK, DARK CLOUDS WITH SILVER LININGS

The storm clouds rolled in so very dangerous
And dark. And upon everything they touched
They left a mark. They brought Hurricane's
Katrina and Rita roaring through the Gulf. And
In their rage, they left tragedy and devastation;
Taking some lives: decimating homes and
Businesses; leaving human hearts raw, ragged,
Scarred, and in pain; causing extra ordinary
Suffering and need - a terrible colossal tragedy
Indeed. Our hearts were so seriously troubled -
Theirs were painfully broken.

Then the dark clouds with beautiful silver linings
Started billowing in and brightly shining. Americans
Began to perform acts of love, courage, mercy and
kindness.

An avalanche of emergency care and supplies were
Donated by government workers, and millions of
Volunteers working through relief agencies, private
Individuals, church groups, hospitals, businesses,
Schools, colleges and shelters - to name just a few.

A Potpourri Collection

All the helpers and workers gave exhaustive
Amounts of time, effort, possessions, and good
Will to the broken and to the weary. Their very
Great compassion was demonstrated through action.

And finally there are dark clouds with silver linings
Yet to be revealed: as the resilient and tough
Victims of the hurricanes demonstrate the strength
Of the human spirit; as they keep going in the midst
Of despair; and as they begin to have great and noble
Dreams of building a future, with great pride. As
They set about recovering, rebuilding or relocating,
Many have asked that we remember them to our God
Through prayer. And so we fervently pray for God's
Mercy and care in the challenges that continue to lie
Ahead!

Psalm 30:5 (NIV)
"...weeping may remain
for a night, but rejoicing
comes in the morning."

A MODERN INVENTION OF AROUND A CENTURY AGO

Have you ever used a wagon,
Equipped with steel rimmed wheels
As a means of transportation?

Sometimes it did beat walking
Or riding a horse – all depending
On the distance and/or the horse's
Disposition.

But then there was one main
Drawback to the wagon means of
Travel. Did I mentioned the steel
Rimmed wheels?

We all understand that road surfaces
Must accommodate to the unyielding
Steel rather than vice versa.

Each passenger painfully felt every
Rock, dent, valley and bump in that
Graveled road.

A Potpourri Collection

Needless to say some bruises, at the
Very least, demanded attention and
At the most encouraged a new
Invention. And was that invention
"Wow – Wow – Whee – Hallelujah!"
Welcomed!

It was the grand replacement of
Steel rimmed wheels with rubber tires.
While riding in that new styled
Faithful wagon we even arrived
Home mostly pain free and in
Time for supper. And so help me,
Even the horses' disposition did
Seem to improve.

Word soon got around about those
New fangled tires and their real as
Well as their exaggerated attributes.

I guess it's just a very loveable trait
Of human nature that we do become
Excited about new inventions
Created by God's humans.

✝ *Ecclesiastes 3:1 (NIV) "There is*
a time for everything, and a season for
every activity under heaven:"

"HELLO AGAIN"

Today I saw her again.
My heart's desire for this reunion was
So keen that the anticipation was painful.

During the separation, thoughts of her
Were continuous - at first wonderful,
Warm, and exhilarating. Then as the separation
Lengthened, bittersweet and longing.

At last it was time to make that trip to travel
Back to see her. I cannot recall the flight:
Just my heart and mind filed with anxious,
Urgent expectations!

But as long as my memory is capable of
Performing, I shall remember the moment
When the back door opened. She stood there
For one second motionless, and I saw her again!

Her expression was so special, so intense, and
So very sincere. Registered on that beautiful,
Mobile, precious face was the exquisite feelings
Shared by the two of us "Hello, again!"

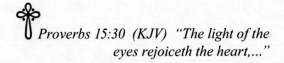

Proverbs 15:30 (KJV) "The light of the eyes rejoiceth the heart,..."

THE SWINGING "SWANG"

I remember: there's nothing like the swings in
The park. Swinging on the swing is such a lark.
You just want to keep swinging until it's dark.
The swings go so high you find yourself
Reaching for the sky. And you hang on so tight
With all of your might, lest you find yourself
In a real fright, falling all the way out of sight.

As the swing slices through the summer air, it
Travels away up there then swiftly back again,
Your emotions to ensnare. It takes you further
Down memory lane when children took turns
Swinging in the "swang," and young mothers
Pushed their youngsters in and out, in and out,
In response to the wee one's pleading shout!

The years fly away. The young mother
Grows old. Now she sways back and forth,
Back and forth, in her cushioned rocking chair:
And listens for her grown-up children's tread
On the stair: then she eagerly waits as they
Step in and out, in and out: listening to their
Mothers hesitant voicing of needs - as they
Honor her by folding her in their loving care.

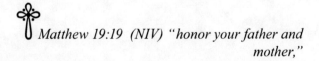 *Matthew 19:19 (NIV) "honor your father and mother,"*

DRAMATIC DREAMS VERSUS TRIUMPHANT REALITY

He dreamed of many degrees
In the world of education.
He lived a life that supplied
Him with a great wealth of useful
Information.

He dreamed of a job involving
Some power and intrigue.
He lived a job of rich service
Meeting many and many a precise
Need.

He dreamed of a trophy wife, who
Would decorate his life.
He lived with a wife filled with
Wisdom, grace, honor, and charm -
Gladly displaying her on his arm.

He dreamed of raising children
Who would follow his deep
Longings. He raised children who
Had a great flair for living life in a
Way showing care, filling him with
Pride, from deep inside.

He dreamed of living in a castle rare.
He lived his life in a real home
Filled with tender love and devotion -
Which took up residence there.

While musing about life's experiences
He sent up fervent thanks to his God
For having granted him triumphant
Realities, instead of dramatic dreams!

(Note: When composing this poem I saw my God in how he often leads our lives in a wonderful way contrary to our own expectations.)

Psalm 19:21 (NIV)
"Many are the plans in a man's heart,
but it is the Lord's purpose that
prevails."

A PAST TIME OF LIFE AND ACTIVITY

Often on a beautiful spring day,
We pass by the crumbling ruins
Of an old home place.
There in the yard space is a
Row of early March flowers.
In their brilliant yellows, they
Are dressing up the landscape.

We consider, with awe,
That in some distant past
There had been human life there.
There had been activity there.
Most likely there had been
A woman there, who gloried in
Floral beauty for her family.

Perhaps her husband planted
The Daffodil bulbs. And when
His wife praised his work,
He felt so proud and powerful.
He knew he could do wonders,
As long as she was by his side!

And when that mother received
Love offerings of colorful flowers,
All for her pleasure, from the tight
Fists of their small and joyful brood;
She knew that husband and children
Gave her wealth beyond measure!
And she became even more dedicated
To the joy and pleasure that comes
Along with love and beauty.

Thanks to whoever once called
This space, "My home-place",
Today you have put a smile on
Many a face and a bit of splendor in
Many hearts!

Song of Solomon 2:11-12 (NCV) "Look, the winter is past; the rains are over and gone. Blossoms appear through all the land. The time has come to sing."

MY LOYAL FRIEND

You are my friend.
And I do treasure you so.
We cherish each other
As only friends can know.

We share our sorrows and joys.
We attend to each others needs.
We share our failures and successes.
We are familiar with each others deeds.

Though you understand me so well,
You still champion me always.
I can count on your priceless loyalty.
It means more than words can tell.

We share good times together: shopping
Camping, hunting, movies, and golfing –
You name it! When shared with my friend,
I never want those times to end.

And so, daily I give thanks for you
My treasured friend!

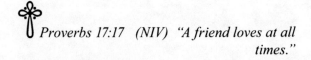

Proverbs 17:17 (NIV) "A friend loves at all times."

THE EMPEROR'S NEW CLOTHES
(Presented by Hickman County High School
Faculty and Staff, Sept 20, 2005)

Wow! What a sight! It turned those forty
Plus performers into bright stars overnight
We thought we knew that story. But we had
Never before seen it portrayed in all its glory.
Those actors and actresses strutted their stuff
As they marched and pranced onto that stage.
We couldn't seem to get enough.
They were hilarious as they entertained us.
We roared our applause and gave standing
Ovations while we guffawed, tittered, grinned
And chuckled.

Never again will we think of "The Emperor's
NEW clothes." in the same OLD way. Nor
Will we think of Faculty and Staff in the same
OLD way. But rather we will remember that
evening in September when while together
working their unique magic, they gave us a
special night to remember as they demonstrated
the result of creativity, talent, hard work and
good will. With gratitude we hold them in our
thoughts and hearts!

*Ecclesiastes 3:1 and 4 (NIV) "There is
a time for everything,....a time to laugh,..."*

Manda Tarkington
Nov. 15, 2010
90th Birthday

SECTION 7

Meet The Author

WILMA ARMSTRONG HUDGINS

Wilma Armstrong Hudgins is the product of a home where dedicated Christian parents taught her to aim high, work hard, honor her commitments and trust in her God.

When Wilma was a preschooler her Dad was a tenant farmer in Hickman County, Tennessee working for less than one dollar per day. Her Mom was a stay-at-home Mom declaring, "Your Daddy and I never graduated from high school but *you* child will graduate from college." Her Mom never wavered from that determination.

After Wilma earned a BS degree from David Lipscomb College in Nashville, Tennessee she discovered that school was "her thing." She later earned an MA degree from George Peabody College in Nashville, Tennessee and a Specialist in Arts. Degree from Eastern Michigan University located in Ypsilanti, Michigan.

While still a young single woman Wilma worked for the FBI in Washington, D.C. for about four years.

Meet The Author

Upon returning to Hickman County in Middle Tennessee she married a southern Christian gentleman, who was a World War II veteran, and a lover of God and humanity. He became a part-time preacher and an elder in the church.

They raised three children, James, Timothy and Melanie who are each talented in their own special ways, both professionally and at home. They are married to loving and loveable mates. They have given to Wayne and Wilma six grandchildren and one step-grandchild, all of whom are, of course, "geniuses." If you doubt that, just ask Wilma about her grandchildren, and when you have the time to listen she will gladly fill you in on more information than you ever even wanted to know!

Wilma is a retired public school teacher, having taught some thirty-two years in Tennessee, Kentucky and Michigan.

She finds tremendous pleasure, joy and satisfaction in her family, her friends, her privilege of teaching Bible classes in Sunday School, and writing poetry, which is published in the the Hickman County Times.

Wilma believes life to be a daily journey with God. She deals with this conviction in her writing and daily prays for His guidance.

Proceeds from this book will be contributed to Tennessee Children's Home in Spring Hill, TN and to medical and spiritual mission work in El Salvador.

Printed in the United States
78141LV00003B/133-261